EXPLORING THE PAST

EXPLORING
PEOPLE

Ralph Whitlock

Wayland

Exploring the Past

Exploring Buildings
Exploring Clothes
Exploring Farming
Exploring Industry
Exploring People
Exploring Transport

Editor: Nick Wallwork
Designer: David Armitage
Cover picture: Family portraits were popular in Victorian times.

First published in 1987 by
Wayland (Publishers) Ltd
61 Western Road, Hove
East Sussex BN3 1JD, England

British Library Cataloguing in Publication Data

Whitlock, Ralph
   People. – (Exploring the past)
   1. Historiography – Juvenile literature
   I. Title   II. Series
   907'.2   D13

   ISBN 1–85210–005–2

Phototypeset by Kalligraphics Ltd, Redhill, Surrey
Printed in Italy by G. Canale & C.S.p.A., Turin
Bound by the Bath Press, Avon

Contents

1 What is the past?   4

2 Questions to ask   6

3 A chronological chart   11

4 Family trees   18

5 Family history   21

6 Names   27

7 Deeper into history   32

8 Unwritten history   36

9 Folklore   40

10 From past to future   43

    Places to visit   45

    Further reading   45

    Glossary   46

    Index   48

1 What is the past?

Is the past the time when our grandparents were young? Or what happened hundreds of years ago? Or what happened yesterday? Or what happened an hour ago?

It is all the past.

Try thinking about the past. What happened yesterday? Write a short account of what happened to you. How do you know about it? Of course, you *remember*!

This book is all about people in the past. It is about how they lived, what they said, what they ate, what they thought about, where they slept, how they spent their leisure time – everything about them.

Horse-racing was a very popular form of entertainment for both rich and poor in Victorian times.

We can, of course, learn about people in the past by reading about them in books. We have to do that when we explore the distant past. To start with, however, it is better to look at the recent past, at people who are still alive and whom we know. That way we can do more exploring on our own.

Let us start by talking to older people in our own family. Our parents and aunts and uncles. If we have grandparents living near us that is even better, because they have seen greater changes during their lives, and we are exploring how things have changed. Perhaps if none of our relations are available we can talk with older neighbours. There will surely be someone we can talk to no matter where we live, someone who remembers about the past.

Old people will always have some interesting memories to share with you.

2 Questions to ask

Once you have found someone to answer your questions, what do you ask them? Prepare a list of questions beforehand. Write them out and be sure to leave room for your notes after each one. If you are able to use a tape recorder it will be most helpful.

Do not try to get everything into one conversation. You will find that when older people begin to remember what happened long ago, one thing will lead to another. They will say, 'Oh, that reminds me . . .' and will start talking about something different from the question you have asked. Let them carry on talking and write down what they tell you. You can go back to your original question later.

Your grandparents may have had a brass bedstead in their bedroom when they were children.

Children's fashions were unknown at the beginning of this century. These children's clothes are very similar to their parents'.

Here are some ideas for questions to ask. When you wrote down what you did yesterday you probably started by writing, 'I got up at half-past seven.' The older person you are talking to no doubt started the day by getting out of bed, so your first question could be:

● 'What sort of bed did you sleep in?' It may have been a feather bed with a brass bedstead. You could then go on to other questions, like:

● 'Could you get hot water from a tap?' Perhaps you will find they had to heat water in a kettle on a kitchen stove.

● 'What did you have for breakfast?'

● 'What did you wear? People seem to have worn more clothes than we do. . . .' Perhaps they will have photographs of themselves as children.

● 'What lessons did you have at school?' Probably not such interesting lessons as you have.
● 'What games did you play?' If an unfamiliar game is mentioned, ask how it was played.

It would be interesting to find out where your ancestors lived. Was it in a row of houses like the one in this picture?

'Where did you live?' This is a question in several parts, because we want to know the name of the town or village and where it is. Also what sort of house it was. Was it a terraced house or a cottage or an apartment over a shop or a big house in the country?

'Did you have electricity or gas in your house?'

'Did you have a radio or television set?' The answer will depend largely on the age of the person concerned.

'Did you travel about much?' If the person happened to belong to a family with a military background you may have a long answer to this question. But if they lived a more settled life, ask whether they had a bike or whether the family had a car. And whether they often made journeys by bus or train, or perhaps tram.

'Did you go on summer holidays?' You may be surprised at how many did not.

'What sort of presents did you receive on your birthday?'

Public transport has changed greatly over the years. This picture shows the new motorized trams taking over from the horse-drawn trams for speed and comfort.

- 'How much pocket-money did you get?'
- 'Did you ever go to hospital?'
- 'Was it very painful to have a tooth out?'
- 'Did you ever learn to play a musical instrument?'
- 'Did you go to Sunday school or church?'
- 'What did you do on winter evenings?'

Asking all these questions will take up several interviews, especially if you put them to several people. When you have all the answers you will find that you have a very interesting picture of what life was like when your grandparents were young. You will have discovered that in many ways it was very different from your life.

Many children learned to play musical instruments to entertain their family.

3 A chronological chart

Now is the time to fit all the information you have gathered into a time scale, or chronology. This is how you set about it.

Mark three vertical columns on a large sheet of paper, with a narrow fourth column on the left-hand side for the dates.

The date at the top will be the year AD 1990. The scale will depend on the size of the paper, but you may find it convenient to allow five or six centimetres for every ten years. Draw lines across the paper to mark the end of each ten years.

In the first column you write in the events in your own life and that of your family. The second column is for local events. The third column is for events of international importance.

Here is an example.

	My family	Local events	National events
1990			
1984			
1983	I started primary school.		Prince William was born.
1982			The Falklands War occurred.
1980		Our new school was built.	Prince Charles and Princess Diana were married.
1979	Sam, my dog, was born.		
1978	I was born.		
1977			Queen's Silver Jubilee.
1975	My parents were married.	The making of the new motorway across the fields began.	
1973	My cousin Mary was born.		Miners went on strike.
1971	My Grandad's house caught fire.		

You can find out what happened on the day you were born by looking at a newspaper printed on that day. Your local newspaper office should have a copy of the paper printed on the day or week of your birth in its library. If you would like a copy of a national newspaper you can write to:

British Newspaper Library
Collindale Avenue
London W9

You will be charged a small fee for each page you order, but you will only need the front page.

To go back to the days when your grandparents were young you will need several sheets of paper. It would be a good idea to take your chart back to the beginning of the twentieth century. Then in your third column you will be able to enter the main world events, which will probably include the two world wars, several coronations, royal weddings and royal jubilees, the landing of

Your grandparents may be able to remember how they celebrated Queen Elizabeth II's coronation.

the first man on the moon and the date when the first men stood on the top of Mount Everest. To find out about these events you will need to look up a history book in your school or local library.

For local events in your second column you will also need to consult your local library. You will probably find that it has a list of important

At 11.30 am on 29 May, 1953, Norgay Tenzing (shown on the right) and Sir Edmund Hillary became the first men to set foot on the summit of Mount Everest.

local events, though there may be gaps for you to fill in from other sources later.

In the first column you enter your family events. If your parents were married in the 1970s it is quite likely that your grandparents were married in the 1950s. They were therefore probably born not long before the Second World War (1939–45) and so lived their schooldays in wartime. This gives added interest to all the answers you have got from them. They were not living in normal times. Everything was disrupted by war. They will remember the bombing of cities, seeing air battles in the sky, perhaps being evacuated to strange places in the country, and all the problems of food and clothes being rationed. Older people may even remember the First World War (1914–1918).

During the Second World War thousands of people sheltered from German bombing in the London Underground.

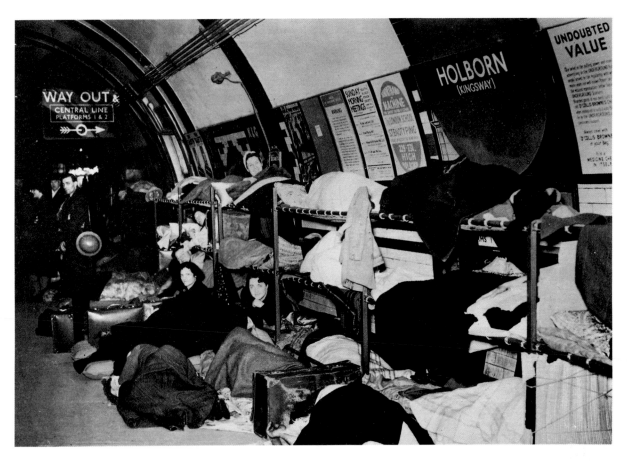

Right Vladimir Lenin was one of the leaders of the Russian Revolution in 1917.

Below In the 1960s the Beatles' music was enjoyed by people all over the world.

When you consult history books you will find yourself reading about people who helped to make history; people such as Winston Churchill, Adolf Hitler, Vladimir Lenin, Neil Armstrong, Sir Edmund Hillary, Emily Pankhurst, Mahatma Gandhi, President Kennedy, Bernard Shaw, The Beatles, Amy Johnson, King Edward VIII, Einstein

John Kennedy became the youngest ever president of the USA in 1961. He prepared many civil rights reforms before his assassination in 1963.

and Picasso. Read about what they did and fit them into your chart. Ask your relatives if they can remember these famous people. They will certainly be able to tell you about some of them.

A number of organizations erect plaques to famous people. The one on the left was erected by the Society of Arts.

You may also ask them about important local people, to be fitted into your second column. Perhaps your town has an impressive city hall. In the entrance you will find a commemorative stone bearing an inscription such as, 'This foundation stone was laid on 1 November, 1955, by the Lord Mayor, Alderman Geoffrey Mason.' This will be another date for you to enter in your chart.

This plaque in Baker Street, London, shows the house where the fictional detective Sherlock Holmes was supposed to have lived.

Some boroughs ('burghs' in Scotland) put up blue plaques on certain houses, which tell you about the famous people who once lived there. The plaques will give the dates, but to find out about the people and what they did you will need to look at history books in the library.

17

4 Family trees

You now have a lot of information about your own family. You have noted the date when you were born and the dates when your brothers and sisters were born. You have marked many other dates, such as the birthdates of your father and mother, of your grandparents and when they were married. By going back to the beginning of the century you will have to fit in some deaths as well.

Now is the time to construct a family tree. You have two parents, four grandparents, eight great-grandparents and sixteen great-great-grand-parents, and so on. Let us suppose your name is John Smith and that your father and his father and his grandfather were also named John Smith. Also that each John Smith was twenty-five years old when his son, the next John Smith was born. You must start your family tree as shown in the small picture on the right.

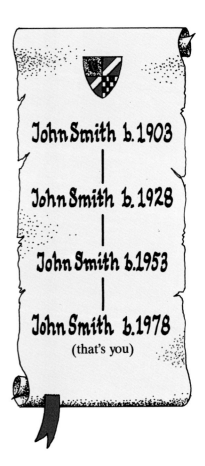

John Smith b. 1903

John Smith b. 1928

John Smith b. 1953

John Smith b. 1978
(that's you)

This is a simple family tree, showing only the direct ancestors on your father's side. For a proper family tree you want to know how other members of the family fit in. There are grandmothers as well as grandfathers, and aunts, uncles, brothers, sisters and cousins. We need to record how they all fit in. So let us start again with the John Smith who was born in 1903. As you can see in the family tree opposite, he married in 1926 and had three children. If you fit all his descendants together on a single sheet of paper you have a family tree of that side of your family. But that is only one part of the family.

The same sort of family tree can be compiled

for your mother's family, the Chalmers, and for your grandmother's family, the Abbotts. It will require a big sheet of paper to compile a complete family tree of all your families back to the beginning of the century, but it can be done. All families of dukes and earls and other nobles do it. The Royal Family can trace their family tree back for over a thousand years. In fact, several generations back, one set of the Queen's ancestors

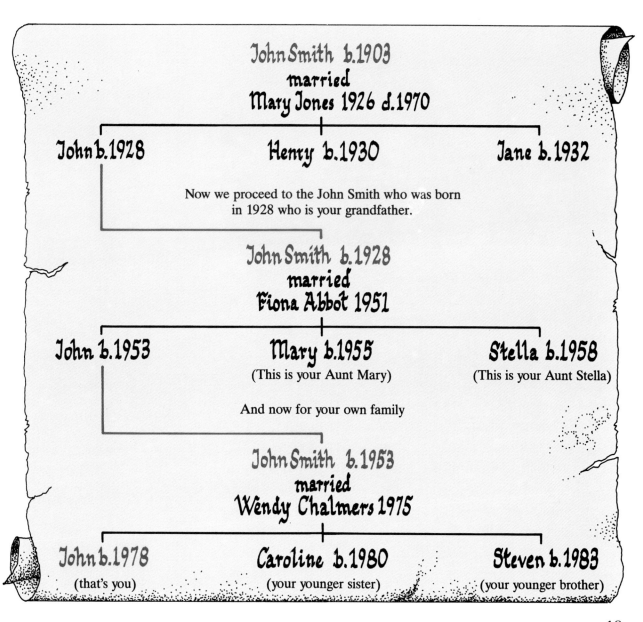

John Smith b.1903
married
Mary Jones 1926 d.1970

John b.1928   Henry b.1930   Jane b.1932

Now we proceed to the John Smith who was born in 1928 who is your grandfather.

John Smith b.1928
married
Fiona Abbot 1951

John b.1953   Mary b.1955   Stella b.1958
            (This is your Aunt Mary)   (This is your Aunt Stella)

And now for your own family

John Smith b.1953
married
Wendy Chalmers 1975

John b.1978   Caroline b.1980   Steven b.1983
(that's you)   (your younger sister)   (your younger brother)

It is widely believed that genetic features such as twins can be passed down through a family.

were named Smith! You may even find that you are related to some famous people. The further back you trace your ancestors the more likely that will be.

Look at any photographs of your family that you have collected. Can you detect a family likeness? Do you look like your father or mother or some other relation? Are there any special characteristics in any branch of the family, such as red hair or a big nose? Is there any tradition of members of the family doing the same sort of work, such as working on the railway or being merchant seamen? Is there a tradition of them being good at a particular sport? Are many of them left-handed? Are there twins or triplets? These things often run in families.

5 Family history

In compiling your family tree you may find that your parents or grandparents do not know the dates of your great-grandparents' births and marriages. You will have to look them up. When you go back further, into the nineteenth and eighteenth centuries, you may have to search hard to discover the facts you want.

Here are some of the possible sources of information. Many of them will be available in your local library.

● Parish registers. These record all the baptisms, marriages and deaths in a parish. Some, but not all, go back as far as the sixteenth century. Many of them are kept, for safety, in county archives, but a number of them have been photographed on microfilm and your library may have a copy.

● All births, marriages and deaths have to be

Some gravestones give interesting background information to local and national history.

registered at the local registry office, and you can obtain a copy there. However, you will have to pay a fee, so only go there if you cannot obtain the information elsewhere.

● Post Office directories. These are published periodically and record the names and occupations of the chief residents and tradesmen in a town.

● Old newspapers and references in local history books can be helpful, though usually only to provide additional details to information you already have.

● Gravestones in churchyards; inscriptions in churches.

● Censuses are conducted by the government

During your research in graveyards you may come across some interesting gravestones, such as this one in Hampstead cemetery.

every ten years. They began in Great Britain in 1801, but the early ones are not very informative. Really detailed censuses began in 1841. They give for each person, the name, address, age and relationship to the head of the family (usually the father of the family), occupation, place of birth and so on. The censuses are compiled on a parish basis, so you will need to know which parish you live in and its boundaries on a map.

Here is a copy of a page of the 1851 census for a village in southern England.

Parish or Township		Ecclesiastical District of		City of Borough of			Town of		Village of	

No. of house-holder's Schedule	Name of Street, Place, or Road, and Name or No. of House	Name and Surname of each Person who abode in the house on the NIGHT of the 30th March 1851	Relation to Head of Family	Condition	Age of		Rank, Profession or Occupation	Where Born	Wheather Blind or Deaf and Dumb
					Males	Females			
27.		Charles Bray	Head	Widower	30		Ag. Lab.	Frobrey? Wiltshire	
		Charles Clarke	Son-in-Law		15		Ag. Lab.	Downton, Wiltshire	
28.		Charles King	Head	Widower	71		Farmer of 150 acres employing 10 Labs.	Winterslow	
		Herbert King	Son	Unmarried	21		Employed at Home	Winterslow	
		Ann Barber	Servant	Unmarried		40	House Servant	Winterslow	
29.		Thomas Judd	Head	Married	46		Groom	Winterslow	
		Mary Judd	Wife	Married		46		Chilmark, Wiltshire	
		William Judd	Son	Unmarried	20		Shoemaker	Winterslow (Master)	
		Praxcel Judd	Daughter	Unmarried		17		Winterslow	
		Thomas Judd	Son		12			Winterslow	
		Elizabeth Judd	Daughter			11	Scholar	Winterslow	
		Harriet Judd	Daughter			9	Scholar	Winterslow	
		Mary Judd	Daughter			8	Scholar	Winterslow	
		Dianna Judd	Daughter			3	Scholar	Winterslow	
30.		Charles Wheelar	Head	Married	38		Farmer of 182 acres employing 6 Labs.	Winterslow	
		Maria Wheelar	Wife			33		Sombourne, Hampshire	
		Sarah Young	Mother-in-Law			60	Annutant	Winchester	
31.		Mary Clarke	Head	Widow		73	Laundress	Winterslow	
		Christian Clarke	Daughter	Unmarried		26	Laundress	Winterslow	
32.		Richard Judd	Head	Married	55		Ag. Lab.	Winterslow	
		Sarah Judd	Wife	Married		63		Winterlow	
		Thomas S. Judd	Son	Unmarried	20		Bricklayers Lab.	Winterslow	
		George Dear	Lodger	Unmarried	20		Ag. Lab.	Winterslow	

Supposing you have found that the grandfather of the first John Smith on your family tree was born around 1851 and you know the name of the place where the family was living. You look up the census and find that he was then a baby a few months old. It tells you the names of his parents and so takes you back even further into the past.

If you have a fairly common surname you may find that a family history society has already done a lot of work for you. Your local library will be able to tell you whether there is a family history society for your name in the district. You should find their information most helpful.

If you study parish registers you will find that before about 1840 many of the women who got married could not sign their names. Someone signed for them and they marked the signature with a cross, thus 'Susan Temple, her mark, x'.

This colourful coat of arms belongs to Winston Churchill's family.

George IV.

Coats of arms bear many symbols and even the colours used are significant. George IV was the King of Great Britain from 1820–30. This is his family crest. See if you can find out the meaning of some of the symbols.

A hundred years earlier many of the men could not sign either. And several hundreds of years ago most people could not read or write.

During this time important people could be identified by the shields and coats of arms they carried. One noble family might have, for instance, a shield with three leopards on it, another might have a black cross. When an important marriage occurred between these two families the shield of the eldest son would bear three leopards on one half and a black cross on the other. So the shields served as a kind of family tree.

A family map

There are always people moving from one area or from one country to another. In the late eighteenth century many people in Britain moved into the new factory-towns from the countryside in search of jobs. Families that had lived in the same area for years were suddenly scattered all over the country. In the 1980s many people are moving from the north of the country to the south where there are more jobs.

Trace an outline map of your country from an atlas. Mark where you were born and any other places where you have lived before your present home.

Mark each place with the dates when you lived there and join them up in correct order. Add arrows and your initials to the line.

Now add lines for your parents, grandparents and as many generations as you can. Use different colours for each generation. Some families may need to use a world outline map.

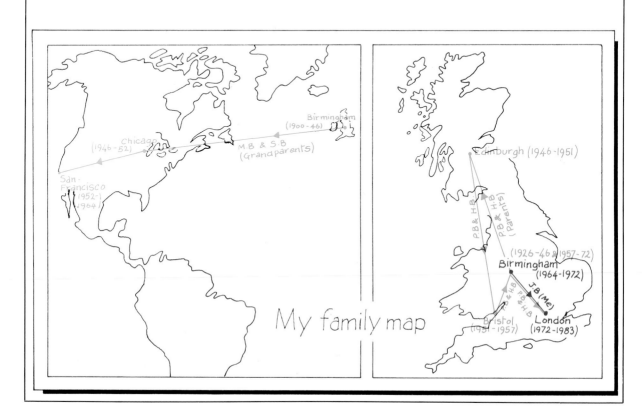

My family map

Birmingham (1900-46)

Chicago (1946-52)

M.B & S.B (Grandparents)

San Francisco (1952-1964)

Edinburgh (1946-1951)

P.B & H.B (Parents)

Birmingham (1964-1972) (1926-46 & 1957-72)

J.B (Me)

Bristol (1951-1957)

London (1972-1983)

6 Names

In the section on family trees the name John Smith is used because Smith is the most common surname in Britain. The reason is that at one time there used to be a smith in every village. If his forename was John he would be known as John the Smith, or John Smith. There would probably also have been John the Carpenter, Robert the Brewer, William the Farmer, Francis the Mason, Peter the Cow-Herd (shortened to Peter Coward), Dennis the Thatcher, Charles the Parson and other people named after the jobs they did. It does, of course, create problems when you try to compile a family tree, because people bearing the same common surname are not necessarily related to one another.

Hundreds of years ago people were named after the jobs they performed or the area they came from. The man in the red hat would probably be called Miller.

Over the years certain Scottish families, or clans, have selected a particular tartan for their family.

Another group of surnames comes from the place where villagers lived. A John who lived at the edge of a wood might be known as John Atwood, or simply John Wood. If he lived near the church he might be called John Church, or if he lived near the castle, John Castle.

Then there were people who were named after their father. John Johnson would be the son of a man named John, James Robinson would be the son of Robin, Peter Nixon would be the son of Nick. The Scottish (Gaelic) word for 'son of' is 'mac', so MacWilliam is really just the same as

Williamson. 'Ap' is Welsh for 'son of', and is usually shortened to just 'p'. So Powell is really Ap-Howell, the son of Howell. A similar rule applies to other languages; in Arabic the word for 'son of' is 'ben'. In the poem about Abou Ben Adhem, the man's name means 'Abou', the son of Adam'.

When families moved to another place the people there would often call them after the place they had come from. John from Newbury would be known as John Newbury, Charles from York would be Charlie York, Henry from London would be Harry London. Claude who came from France would be Claude French, James from Scotland would be James Scott.

This farrier in North Wales still makes horseshoes in the same way that his ancestors did.

Almost everybody in Britain is descended from people who came from other places. The Normans came from Normandy, the Vikings from Norway and Denmark, the Saxons from North Germany and the Romans from Italy. Before them came the Celts from Central Europe. Celtic languages are still spoken in Wales, Scotland and Ireland. Make a note of these people and see if you can find out from a history book when they first arrived and where they settled.

More recently other people have come to Britain to live. They include West Indians, Indians, Chinese, Arabs, Vietnamese and even Tibetans. Do you belong to any of these peoples? Or do any of your friends come from distant countries?

You can guess who your early ancestors may have been from your looks. This blonde-haired, blue-eyed woman may be descended from the Vikings who invaded Britain hundreds of years ago.

***Right** Britain is now a multicultural country. This means that people from many races now live and work here together.*

***Below** This woman is an actress with the Royal Shakespeare Company. Her parents came to Britain in the 1950s when Britain actively encouraged immigration from abroad.*

Make a list of the names of all the people in your class. Using books from your local library see how many names you can find the origin or meaning of. Your parents may be able to help you if you have an unusual name. Listed below are a few examples.

Baxter – a female baker.

Campion or Champion – a professional fighter, a champion.

Farmer – The modern meaning came after the surname. Before that a farmer was a tax-collector, 'farm' once meaning 'firm or fixed payment'.

Fletcher – someone who made and sold arrows

Kellogg – literally 'kill hog', a slaughterer.

Ward – a watchman or guard.

7 Deeper into history

In your talks with older people you may find that some of their memories are not entirely reliable because the events being recalled happened such a long time ago. Check whenever possible.

One such instance concerns an old lady who said that her grandmother was taught needlework by Lord Nelson's sister. When the dates were checked it was found that the grandmother and Lord Nelson's sister were not alive at the same time. Although the memory was in general correct, the teacher was in fact Lord Nelson's niece, not his sister.

You may have had a relative who fought in a famous battle. One woman alive in the 1950s had a medal which her father had won at the Battle of Waterloo in 1815.

Right Many churches and cathedrals allow you to take brass rubbings from memorial tablets.

Below This bust of Karl Marx, the founder of Communism, stands above his grave at Highgate cemetery in London. Perhaps there is a monument in your town to somebody famous.

However, some memories are astonishingly accurate. A lady alive in the 1950s was able to show a medal which her father had won at the Battle of Waterloo in 1815, 140 years earlier. The explanation was that her father was a drummer boy at the battle. He lived a long life, and when he was over seventy he married for the second time. The lady who had the medal was the youngest daughter of the second marriage. Interesting events such as this are known as 'century-spanners'.

Perhaps some famous person lived in your neighbourhood. You may see their portrait in the local library or museum. Or you may be able to visit the house where they lived. It might be interesting to compile their life story. Compare their dates with those on your chart and see how many of your ancestors were alive at the same time and possibly knew him or her.

Going further back into history, you will find monuments and inscriptions to important local people in churches and graveyards. In the Middle Ages it became fashionable to erect brass tablets to their memory in the parish church. You can make brass rubbings of these tablets. The figures shown are rather stylized and not actual portraits, but the costumes are generally accurate. The inscriptions record their names, and you may find that some of the names are still known in the neighbourhood. They may even be the same as your own surname.

In England one of the earliest and most detailed historical documents is the Domesday Book. It was compiled on the orders of King William the Conqueror in 1086 and is a kind of inventory of almost every place in England. Details are given of the owner and size of each place, the population, the mills, the woodlands and pastures and the value of everything. We don't know the names of the peasants and slaves, but the Domesday

The Domesday Book was written in 1086 and provides an important historical background to life at that time.

Book tells us the names of the chief men in each place, how much land they cultivated and how many farm animals they had. No other country has such a detailed survey from so early a date. The Domesday Book is the basis for every local history in England. You should be able to find an edited copy of it in your local library.

In 1986 many schools helped in the preparation of a second Domesday survey of their locality. This was to commemorate the 900th anniversary of the original Domesday Book. Did your school take part?

In the same way a great deal about local life in Scotland over the past 200 years may be found in the first, second and third Statistical Accounts of the Parishes of Scotland. These give details of the landscape, climate, use of land, size of population and the customs and jobs of the people. The first was written around 1790, the second around 1840 and the third, which was begun after the Second World War, is still incomplete.

Details about the people and land of Scotland are recorded in the first, second and third Statistical Accounts of the Parishes of Scotland.

8 | Unwritten history

Before the Domesday Book, documentary history is scarce. In those days few people could read or write, and many of the records that were made have been destroyed by war or accident. Some records do exist back to Saxon times, but they are generally very scrappy.

Where written history fails, archaeology takes over. Archaeologists try to discover details about the past by digging and studying what they find.

Is there an archaeological site in your area? Archaeologists don't just dig anywhere. They choose a site where they know people were living a long time ago. Some of these sites are in towns, many of which have existed in the same place for hundreds of years. When new buildings are being planned the builders first of all demolish the buildings at present on the site so that they

Above *Many important documents were destroyed by air raids during the Second World War.*

Left *Archaeologists at this site in Dover are excavating the ruins of a Roman house.*

Left *Archaeologists spend many hours sifting through dirt and rubble hoping to discover clues as to how people lived in the past.*

Below *This comb made from reindeer bone was discovered near Stonehenge in Wiltshire. It shows us that people have been worried about their looks for centuries.*

can start afresh. Archaeologists are then given a few weeks or months to explore the site. By careful digging they can explore the foundations of earlier buildings and learn something about the lives of people who were living there. These are called 'rescue digs', and are going on in many places. Is there one near you?

The sort of thing archaeologists look for are objects which were thrown away, such as disused tools and broken pottery. Sometimes they find coins and ornaments, especially on sites where early buildings have been destroyed by fire. Every detail has to be carefully recorded. The archaeologist scrapes the soil away carefully with a trowel, or even a spoon, and records where each object was found and how far below the surface. Bones of animals often reveal what kinds of meat the people ate. Broken millstones show that the people ground seeds to make flour and bread.

Archaeologists have even devised methods for identifying grains of pollen, which tell them what trees and other plants flourished in those days. And a new technique, using radio-carbon, enables them to date fairly accurately items five or ten thousand years old.

Excavations in towns usually reveal details of life there over the past thousand years. In Anglo-Saxon England between AD 500 and AD 1000, towns were small and not very numerous, and much of what is known about the period is the result of excavating burials. Pagan Saxon kings were often buried with all their treasure, which included armour, weapons and large amounts of gold and silver. Before the Saxons, Britain was a Roman province for 400 years, and some people lived in well-planned towns or in comfortable country houses. When the Romans invaded Britain in AD 43 they found it occupied by Celtic tribes, very few of whom lived in towns.

This burial mound on Orkney is the resting place of a Viking chieftain

Left *These arrowheads have been cut from pieces of stone. They would have been used for hunting animals for food and clothing.*

There were many other invasions even earlier than this. The Celts, when they arrived, were the first people to know how to smelt iron and to make iron tools and weapons. This gave them a big advantage in war. The time in which they lived is called the Iron Age. The period before that was called the Bronze Age, when bronze tools and weapons were used. It lasted for many hundreds of years. The Bronze Age invaders found the country occupied by people who had only weapons and tools made of stone, so their period is known as the Stone Age. It is divided into three parts: the New Stone Age or Neolithic, the Middle Stone Age or Mesolithic, and the Old Stone Age or Palaeolithic. Neolithic men were the first farmers. They lived in round thatched houses, grew food crops in small fields and kept domestic animals, such as cows, sheep and pigs. Before that, people lived entirely by hunting.

Archaeologists have accumulated a vast amount of information about the people who lived in all these periods. They can tell us what they ate and wore, what diseases they had and how long they lived, but they can never tell us their names. You may be sure, though, that you had ancestors living in those ages.

Below *Archaeologists can date these bronze swords fairly accurately by studying the quality of the metal.*

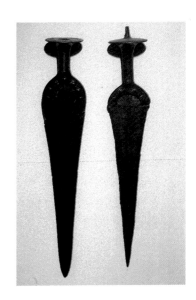

9 Folklore

Folklore is a kind of verbal history. It includes tales that have been handed down from grandparents to grandchildren throughout the centuries. It is also concerned with festivals, holidays, customs and local events.

Most folklore belongs to the time when hardly anyone could read or write. People had to rely on memory. In prehistoric times there were certain classes of priests or bards whose duty it was to memorize things that today we record in writing. They had to learn by heart long lists of kings and their ancestors, pedigrees in the Bible, and also immensely long poems about past

Every spring in Derbyshire, beautiful pictures made from flower petals are erected next to water wells. These well dressings are erected in the hope that God will bless the well and keep the water running from it throughout the summer.

The Morris dancers' stamping dance through the village was performed to wake up the good spirits of the soil so that they would produce a plentiful harvest.

battles and other events, which took days to recite. But when writing was invented, people no longer had to rely so much on their memories, and so our memories are not so good nowadays. We remember just what we want to remember and sometimes we make mistakes.

Have you ever played the game 'Memory' on winter evenings or at parties? You stand or sit in a circle, and one person thinks of a message and whispers it into the ear of the next one. That one passes it on in the same way, and when the last person receives it he or she has to repeat it aloud. It is usually very different from the original message. People often do not listen properly and so make mistakes.

In folklore the story generally has some truth in it, but it isn't safe to rely on the details. Stories change in the telling.

Folklore is, however, important as a link with the very remote past. Are there any interesting customs or legends or festivals in your locality? Are there days when you go in procession around the streets? Or festivals to commemorate some important local event from the past? If so, see if you can find out more about it. Perhaps it involves a dramatic story about which you can make a play at school.

What games do you play at school? Are there some which you never see referred to in books — you just play them? They often involve dances and mimes and chanting rhymes. These are an important part of folklore. Some of them were probably played by children many hundreds of years ago.

The game of ring-a-ring-o'-roses is based on the plague, a disease which spread through England in the seventeenth century killing thousands of people. The sneezes in the rhyme were the first sign that a person had the disease.

10 From past to future

Can you imagine yourself as a grandparent? It is difficult, but your grandparents were once children like you. What do you think *you* will remember to tell your grandchildren? Supposing they were to ask you some of the questions in chapter 2, such as 'What did you wear?' 'What games did you play?' 'Did you go on summer holidays?' 'What presents did you have on your birthday?'; do you think you will be able to remember?

There are a lot of other things which you have noted in your charts and notebooks that you will probably not remember. That is why your written records are important. Think about the things that children may like to know about in twenty or thirty years' time, and then try to make sure that

It is important for you to keep a record of your life so that your descendants can discover how you lived.

Left *The children in this picture will have an exciting record of Princess Diana's visit. They are recording history.*

Below *Every year athletics records are being broken. Do you think that there is a limit to how far humans can improve their performance?*

the information is there waiting for them. Fortunately, there are more ways of preserving information today than in your grandparents' time. There are videos, tapes, slides and computer disks. Make use of them all. Take good care of them, together with your maps, photographs and drawings. What you have been doing is important. You have been recording history.

What do you think life will be like in the future? Studying what you have learned about the past you will notice that people are taller than they used to be. They are also healthier and live longer. Every year athletes are breaking new records and people are inventing new things. But one day everything we now regard as modern will seem old-fashioned! Or will it? What do you think?

Places to visit

Among the places you may usefully visit are:
- your local library.
- your local museum.
- your local newspaper office, where you may be able to look up past files.
- your local historical or archaeological society which you may be able to join, if they have junior membership. You should also enquire (at the library) whether there are any family history societies operating in your neighbourhood.
- local churchyards, cemeteries and churches.
- Jorvik Viking Centre in York, and similar centres elsewhere.

Further reading

Into the Past, a series of four books, by Sallie Purkis (Longman).
Any book you can find on local history. Any book you can find on local folklore. A good general book on folklore is *Folklore, Myths and Legends of Britain* (The Reader's Digest).
Any old maps and atlases.
The Family History Book, by Stella Colwell (Phaidon).
Your Family History by C.M.Matthews (Lutterworth).
Genealogical Research in England and Wales, by Smith & Garner (Bookcraft Publishers).
Scottish Roots, by Alwyn Jones (MacDonald).
Trace Your Ancestors, by L.G.Pine (Evans).
Akenfield, by Ronald Blythe (Allen Lane).
The Tudor Family, by Ann Mitchell (Wayland).
The *Everyday Life* series, by Marjorie and C. H. B. Quennell (Batsford).

Glossary

Archaeology   A study of the past, made by investigating sites and objects, usually by digging.

Bronze Age   A period in history when people used weapons, implements and utensils made of bronze (a mixture of copper and tin).

Census   An official survey of the population, including the recording of details about the people.

Century-spanners   Instances of human memory spanning a hundred years or more.

Chronology   An arrangement of events in a table or chart according to the dates on which they occurred.

Commemorative   Preserving the memory of.

Documentary   Recorded in writing or in some other way, as distinct from reliance on human memory.

Everest, Mount   The highest mountain on Earth, at 8848m.

Excavations   Exploration by digging, usually referring to archaeological digs.

Folklore   Collections of memories of the past concerning the customs, beliefs, traditions and superstitions of ordinary people.

Illiterate   Unable to read or write.

Inscription   Words inscribed on a monument, stone, coin or some similar object.

Iron Age   The era of history when iron weapons and implements were used.

Jubilee   Usually the fiftieth anniversary of an event.

Mesolithic Age   Or the Middle Stone Age; a period of prehistory between the Palaeolithic and Neolithic ages; usually regarded as the period when people began to move from a hunting economy to one based on growing crops and keeping domestic animals.

Monument   Something to commemorate an event or person, usually an inscribed stone or a building.

Neolithic Age   Or the New Stone Age; a period of history, immediately before the Bronze Age, when people had implements and weapons made only of stone and wood.

Palaeolithic Age Or the Old Stone Age; the earliest period of history, when people had only simple stone implements and weapons and lived by hunting.

Pedigree A chart, table or family tree showing descent through a succession of ancestors.

Plaque An ornamental tablet fastened to a wall, usually commemorating a person.

Radio-carbon dating Dating by means of the modern technique of measuring the shedding of atoms by radio-active carbon.

Register An official record of events, such as births, marriages, deaths and school attendances.

Rescue dig An archaeological excavation undertaken on a site needed for buildings or roads.

Stone age The time when humans largely depended on stone tools and weapons; see Mesolithic, Neolithic and Palaeolithic Ages.

Stylized Conventional and somewhat artificial rather than lifelike.

Picture acknowledgements
Brian Jenkins 40; John Sheridan 37 (top & bottom), 38, 39 (top & bottom); Mary Evans 7, 10, 32; Sporting Pictures (UK) Ltd. 48; Topham 6, 8, 12, 13, 15, (lower picture), 16 (lower), 17, 19, 20, 21, 22, 25, 33 (top & bottom), 34, 35, 36, 41, 46; Zefa 5, 20, 42, 43.

Index

Ancestors 8, 18, 19, 20, 29, 33, 39, 40
Archaeology 36–7, 38, 39
   radio-carbon 38
   'rescue digs' 37
Archives 21

Birthdays 9, 18, 43
Births 12, 21, 22, 23, 26
Britain 23, 26, 27, 30, 34, 35, 38
   Roman 30, 38
   Saxon 30, 38
British Newspaper Library 12
Bronze Age 39
Buildings 36, 37

Celts 38, 39
Censuses 23, 24
'Century-spanners' 33
Characteristics 20
Children 6, 7, 10, 18, 43
Chronological chart 11–14, 16, 17, 33, 43
Church 10, 22, 28, 33, 34
   yards 22
Clothes 7, 43
Coats of arms 24, 25
Cousins 18
Customs 40, 42

Dates 14, 17, 18, 31, 32, 35, 38
Deaths 18, 21, 22
Domesday Book 34–5, 36
   900th Anniversary 35

Events 11, 32, 40, 41
   family 11, 14
   international 11, 12, 13
   local 11, 13, 14, 40, 42
   national 11

Family 5, 9, 11, 18, 19, 20, 23, 26, 27, 28, 29
Family history society 24
Family trees 18, 19, 21, 25, 26
First World War 12, 14
Folklore 40, 42
Future, the 43–4

Games 8, 41, 42, 43
Generations 19, 26
Grandchildren 40, 43
Grandparents 4, 5, 6, 10, 12, 14, 18, 21, 26, 32, 40, 43, 44
Gravestones 22, 34
Great-grandparents 18, 21
Great-great-grandparents 18

History 15, 32, 34, 40
   books 5, 13, 14, 22, 30, 31
   documentary 36, 41, 43, 44
   local 17, 35
   unwritten 36
Houses 9, 17, 38, 39

Interviews 6–7, 8–10
Iron Age 39

Jobs 26, 27, 35

Library 12, 13, 17, 21, 24, 31, 33, 35

Maps 23, 26, 44
Marriages 14, 18, 21, 22, 24, 25, 33
Memory 4, 5, 6, 32, 33, 40, 41, 43
Mesolithic 39
Middle Ages 34

Monuments 34

Names 22, 23, 24, 27, 28, 29, 31, 34, 35, 39
Neolithic 39
Newspapers 12, 22
Nobility 19, 25

Occupations 22, 23
Older people 6–7, 32

Paleolithic 39
Parents 5, 14, 18, 20, 21, 24, 26, 28, 31, 33
Parish 21, 23, 34
   church 34
   registers 21, 24
Past, the 4, 5, 24, 36–38, 44
Photographs 7, 20, 21, 44
Plaques 17
Population 34, 35
Post Office directories 22

Reference books 17, 22, 42
Registry office 22
Royalty 12, 19

School 8, 13, 14, 35, 42
Scotland 17, 28, 29, 30, 35
Second World War 12, 14, 35, 36
Shields 25
Sisters 18, 32
Statistical Accounts of the Parishes of Scotland 35

Tools 39
Towns 9, 22, 26, 36, 38
Twentieth century 12, 26, 35

Villages 9, 23, 27, 28, 41

Wales 30
War 14, 33, 36, 40